VANCOUVER *Signature* INTERIORS

Publisher True Worth Publications
Editor Lorraine Demers
Art director and designer Todd Chapman
Hangar 18 Creative Group Inc.
Interior photography Ivan Hunter
Portrait photography Robert Kent

ISBN 0-9738647-0-2

First published in 2008 by
True Worth Publications
120–8211 Sea Island Way
Richmond, British Columbia
Canada V6X 2W3
T 604 232 4059
F 604 232 4049

Distributed internationally by
18 KARAT International Product Sourcing Inc.
5292 - 272nd Street
Langley, B.C.
Canada V4W 1S3
T 1.888.849.8811
www.eighteenkarat.com

Vancouver Signature Interiors
www.vancouversignatureinteriors.com
Printed by Prisma Graphic
Phoenix, Arizona
First printing, 2008

COVER Visionary Living in Yaletown – Above and Beyond

VANCOUVER *Signature* INTERIORS

A **TrueWorth** Publication

CONTENTS

AN INTRODUCTION BY THU WATSON

Sophisticated, sexy and refreshing – Vancouver, Canada has developed a whole new vocabulary to define the essence of what distinguishes it as one of the world's most desirable cities to live in.

What is Vancouver's secret? Is it the enviable climate graced by the air of the Pacific Ocean? Perhaps it's the spectacular natural setting that permits golf and sailing all in the span of a few hours with the backdrop of majestic mountains – not to mention its role as host to the 2010 XXI Olympic Winter Games. It's all this and more – including the warmth of its inhabitants that distinguishes Vancouver as Canada's jewel on the West Coast. It's no wonder Vancouver attracts an influx of newcomers compelled to establish their 'home away from home' in our beautiful and affluent city.

Once a 'newcomer' myself, I am honoured to be Canadian and proud to call Vancouver my home. As a designer of interiors, the splendour of Vancouver's natural elements inspires me to create interiors that reflect our enviable surroundings and illustrate elegant coastal living – defining Vancouver's international signature. It is this love of Vancouver's people and the city itself that inspired me to create this book.

Vancouver Signature Interiors will take you on a journey into the world of a select group of Vancouver's leading designers of interiors. Their innovative style-savvy designs capture the essence of living the West Coast lifestyle to the fullest.
Each distinctive interior is worthy of representing Vancouver's signature on an international scale. Every exquisite design is as unique and individual as their author's personal signature.

Vancouver Signature Interiors invites you to experience some of Vancouver's most luxurious and elegant homes. For those who celebrate the art of living well, let's open the doors to begin this exhilarating adventure. Walk through these pages and share with me these exceptional residences designed for gracious living.

We'll make a grand entrance through the captivating lens of talented photographer, Ivan Hunter. So, join me and step inside *Vancouver Signature Interiors*.

Live well & enjoy —

Thu Watson
Publisher

A FOREWORD BY ROBERT LEDINGHAM

When I first came to Vancouver in 1966, Vancouver was a small city that was blessed, and still is, with one of the world's most beautiful settings – the water, the mountains, the landscape. It was a time when West Coast architects were experimenting with unique expressions of residential architecture tied to the landscape and organic materials. Inside spaces merged with exterior landscapes and the interiors reflected this relationship. It was a period of re-sawn cedar paneling and natural coloured quarry tile. The interior design community consisted of a series of studios on South Granville which in most cases made their own furniture and curtains.

As more interior designers moved West in the seventies, alliances were formed with architectural and office interior firms. Residential work remained in the hands of a series of small design firms or retail establishments. It was an interesting mix of traditional and contemporary styles with a very limited selection of beautiful products. One was constantly looking further afield for exciting new and old furniture, fabrics and accessories.

The world's fair in 1986 brought the world to Vancouver and put the city on the international map. For the next twenty years the urban core changed with the development of many condominiums. With the influx of both Asian and other nationalities, the city blossomed with a wide variety of culinary offerings and retail experiences. The international influence had a profound impact on the urban lifestyle.

The inner core of Vancouver has been transformed with residential towers. What was once a sleepy cityscape now sets trends in urban planning that is studied around the world. This international focus has challenged the interior design field to achieve new heights. Technology and the Internet have brought the world to our doorstep; accordingly the opportunities have been embraced by the design community.

Vancouver Signature Interiors features a diverse group of designers to make the evolving interiors that comprise the West Coast style. Many of the interiors are housed in condominium towers but each shows an individual style in approaching their design solutions. Whether it is a house in West Vancouver that reflects the West Coast indoor/outdoor relationships or a traditional home in Point Grey, each solves these relationships in a different manner. As you turn the pages of this collection, I am sure you will be captured by the spirit of West Coast that is uniquely Vancouver.

Robert Ledingham

Robert Ledingham LEDINGHAM DESIGN CONSULTANTS

World renowned for his contemporary style and modern signature, Robert Ledingham also takes pleasure in renovating a character home.

Ledingham believes good design must express function and project individual style, but it is his disciplined restraint and a keen sense of proportion that go furthest in creating the distinctive "look" that is his. His appreciation for openness in quest of calming effect ensures great unity of space, where flow and unification seamlessly meet function.

Materials are simple, not trendy, the colour scheme is neutral, yet everything is well designed and finely crafted. While following his intrinsic style of a restrained palette, Ledingham admits that in this home as in all his designs, the devil is in the details. He emphasizes the importance of beautiful materials against a neutral palette, so as not to compromise the supreme quality of the design's elegance statement.

Whether through a conservatory that opens onto a terrace, or emulated by floor to ceiling glass tiles evoking the ocean, the outdoors is effortlessly carried indoors. This is signature Ledingham, a West Coast pioneer interior designer consummate at recognizing the significance of reflecting the outdoors in the design elements of the interiors.

With the knowledge and understanding that his task is to complement the architecture of a house or a building, rather than to decorate, Ledingham extends the given architecture and expands on its natural setting. Thus achieving the ultimate expression of design – unity and function.

In their entire splendour and elegance, Ledingham's interiors invite the homeowner to dwell in sumptuous living spaces that remain forever timeless.

PREVIOUS PAGE An elegant two-storey living room overlooks Coal Harbour and the North Shore Mountains. A rich blend of natural beauty and cosmopolitan flavour.

LEFT The rotunda entry hall features an inlaid limestone and marble floor, lit silver leaf ceiling dome and rich mahogany wall paneling.

RIGHT An inviting family room and kitchen is seamlessly integrated with mahogany paneling and graphite finish appliances.

THE GARDEN BOOK
GERHARD RICHTER

LEFT A floating mahogany staircase is backed with a chain mail screen.

RIGHT One of two living room seating areas, anchored by a twelve-foot 'sand pan', both rooms maximize the spectacular views of the cityscape and the mountains.

LEFT The entry hall rotunda leads to the master ensuite through the dressing rooms. The upholstery of the chaise contrasts with the background materials.

ABOVE The powder room retains the uniformity of the interior's high contrast materials of mahogany and limestone.

RIGHT A full height translucent glass wall simulates windows, flooding the master bath with light, while diaphanous flat fabric panels soften the hard surfaces.

LEFT A sitting lounge in the master bedroom is a tranquil oasis offering a bird's eye view of Stanley Park.

RIGHT The understated hotel-style bedding in the master bedroom keeps the décor simple, yet welcoming.

NEXT PAGE Spectacular views of Coal Harbour are showcased by floor to ceiling windows.
At a distance, the landmark Lions Gate Bridge leads to Whistler Mountain.

LEFT The family room is furnished with high back sofas offering a comfortable seating arrangement around the focal points of the fireplace and television. Square painted wood frame panels on the ceilings beautify throughout this Point Grey heritage home.

RIGHT A custom designed metal chandelier anchors the dining room adjacent to the contemporary open-concept kitchen.

LEFT An enclosed veranda with triple hung windows features painted wood wall paneling. A piano serves as a sculptural element relating to the adjacent living room.

RIGHT Triple hung walk-out windows relate the kitchen and the family dining area leading to the exterior dining terrace.

LEFT A formal dining room features an antique English Sheraton dining table and a set of Dutch dining chairs. The elegant gold leaf ceiling and hand carved chandelier create an ambient shimmer.

ABOVE An antique Murano glass vessel complements the colouring and style of the antique marble slab top.

RIGHT The powder room features painted paneling and upholstered walls with a custom design mirror and crystal sconces.

LEFT The master bedroom is graciously swathed in silk, wool carpet and richly upholstered walls, warmed by a 19th century French fireplace.

RIGHT A serene master ensuite viewed from the well-appointed master bedroom which overlooks the garden.

David Christopher

David Christopher FX-40 BUILDING DESIGN

For David Christopher, building is an adventure. The design adventure begins with the constructive synergy drawn from his relationship with his client. As the epic unfolds, together they create something uniquely personal.

The alliance of Christopher's design talents with his client's vision has them both dedicated to learning the dynamics of "living and breathing the process" of designing their home.

An original home design by David Christopher evolves from each of the diverse personalities involved. As such, each residence reflects the client's personal style and Christopher's interpretation of their lifestyle. In the quest for something truly unique, the design ultimately starts from the site, the project requirements, and the needs and desires of the end user – the client.

Christopher believes that the finest homes are the result of the homeowner's innate interaction with their chosen designer, and their flexibility within the relationship to embrace the necessary adjustments as the process unfolds. The most satisfied clients are those who are equally involved in that journey and ultimately its end result.

Along with the challenges come the rewards of maximum design flexibility through evolution. It is this infinite adaptability of design that has seen this master designer create a distinctive portfolio of home styles, from authentic Craftsman, West Coast native lodge and West Coast modern to a prairie-style home, even an East Coast-style beach house. Christopher builds on his client's quest for something original, takes the intangible, turns it into an idea, and finally a structure emerges – a structure with flow and character that is customized for the family who will ultimately make this house their home.

It is the adventure through synergy created between David Christopher and his clients that ultimately assures the successful completion of his exclusive home designs.

PREVIOUS PAGE This Yaletown condo features a dynamic mixture of geometric forms and modern materials above expansive views of False Creek. The living room features a stainless steel clad cylindric support column complementing the circular stainless steel inlay of the fireplace hearth.

LEFT The inward curve of the custom dining room wall complements the kitchen's cylindrical display structure.

RIGHT A reflective mirror application innovatively dissembles a square structural column.

PREVIOUS PAGE LEFT The kitchen cabinetry and the media centre feature exotic Anigre veneers maximizing continuity and visual spatial expansion.

PREVIOUS PAGE RIGHT Open-concept living spaces reveal sweeping views of False Creek.

LEFT Horizontal grained walnut panels in the raised walkway lead to the bedrooms.

CENTER The curvature of the millwork frames the vanity mirror of the powder room.

RIGHT The guest bedroom is furnished with a custom leather-upholstered headboard. A circular motif completes the tailored geometric scheme.

PUTMAN STYLE
Ron Arad

Alda Pereira ALDA PEREIRA DESIGN

Clean and harmonious décors define Alda Pereira's inspired interiors. Adventures in space distinguish this fine home specialist.

Uncomplicated, livable and ultimately functional, Pereira's interior designs embrace both the warm and cool contrasts that are indigenous to the West Coast and the lifestyle they dictate. She brings an appreciation of the outdoors through consummate use of raw materials and eloquent lighting.

Rooms are designed to adjust with a family's evolving needs over time. The variation of vibrant or muted hues of blues and greens of the décor reflect the nuances of the ocean's mood in the presence of the imposing mountains. The result is a serene and calming effect, comforting to all residents.

With a delicate, yet stately balance, the outside influences of nature's Feng Shui flow throughout the house. Within, yin meets yang, portraying both the strong masculinity and the fragile femininity of life. Masculine elements manifest in angular lines – a long and lean sideboard, tucked into an alcove, a feature fireplace, and solid materials such as concrete and steel. The sexy transitions from masculine to sensual feminine are heightened as staircase windows open to the evening skies above. The warm wood tones and glass are evocative of the earth's simplicity.

Pereira's signature as an award-winning designer is her inventive and open approach – her ability to introduce natural elements to the interior space of the family home, assimilating materials that withstand the passage of time.

PREVIOUS PAGE A highly functional and livable kitchen and family room overlook Deep Cove and the North Shore Mountains.

LEFT Large limestone tiles throughout the main floor complement the Afromosia millwork details, reflective of the indigenous warm and cool contrasts of the West Coast.

RIGHT Family room workstations boast spectacular North Shore views. The sensitivity to sightlines throughout lends an intimate privacy to the family room, enhanced by the subtle warmth of the colour scheme.

PUTMAN STYLE
Ron Arad

LEFT Expert use of raw materials adds stately balance to the stairwell, featuring Afromosia risers, limestone slab treads and custom tinted concrete walls.

RIGHT A gracious guest suite features Wenge millwork, complemented by a richly hued glass mosaic in the bathroom.

Gilmour's got a machete mouth
THE MAIN PRO BLEM IS YOU R
and a penchant for the double cross
Creator of FUNDAMEN TAL IDEA
IT HAS NO PHILO SOPHICAL PREMISE WHATSOEVER
the artist follows a relent less upward
THE WORK IS MERELY A SERIES OF
progress: a virtuoso study in human
COM PLETELY SENSE LESS EPISODES
that manages to be hilariously appauling
yet deeply com passionate
BUT WHAT IS THE ARTISTS REAL INTENTIONS?
Bril liantly ef fe ctive Gilmore
TO MAKE US THINK? TO FRIGHTEN US?
is a conquest ado r of the gutter
F ROM THE VERY OPEN ING
His vision IS vitriolic
never dull He is still the quintessencial painter
of the north
heal Shot through
with deadly accuracy

LEFT The guest bedroom featuring crafted millwork is modern in its simplicity of form and function.

RIGHT The lower level spa features white Statuario marble and hand-hewn volcanic mosaic tile.

LEFT A subtle colour scheme harmonizes the romantic lines of the master bedroom.

ABOVE A Damask print is etched on frameless glass panels.

RIGHT The master ensuite features French marble – a statement of timeless elegance.

Ted Feenstra FEENSTRA ARCHITECTURE INC.

Architect Ted Feenstra is renowned for his open approach to thoughtful interior design. True to West Coast architecture's reverence for its spectacular natural setting, Feenstra's work is enriched by the dramatic vistas – ocean, trees, and light.

Feenstra is a contemporary specialist who takes a clean fresh approach, where space, colour, finishes and furnishings work symbiotically to evoke an atmosphere that is dramatic and comfortable. He advocates the use of traditional elements in modern applications. The innovative functions of materials such as glass and granite and the effects of contrasting blacks and whites render timeless designs.

Feenstra introduces the outdoors to interior spaces wherever possible through the use of both elemental and refined materials. Indoor spaces make an easy transition to outdoors, onto the deck of a condominium or the landscaping of a house. Inside, the fireplace is reinterpreted by linear gas flames, encased horizontally. These streamlined modern materials replace the wood-burning fireplace of our childhood, but the result remains a focal point for gracious living.

He encourages his clients to make use of their space according to their lifestyle and to embrace a palette of colour that expresses their personality.

Feenstra's signature is a celebration of the minimalist approach to interior design – contemporary, mono-neutral, clean and simplified. The results are sanctuary and calm in counterbalance to the hectic pace of city living.

PREVIOUS PAGE This exceptional penthouse offers 360° views accentuated by the dramatic three storey vaulted ceiling. The glass and steel spiral stairway allows easy access to the amenities of the roof terrace.

LEFT Sculpted walls and ceiling featuring luminescent fiber optics flank the over-height living area.

RIGHT The wine room's warm ambiance balances the glass and steel of the spiral stairway.

SEQUENCE The powder room's chameleon lighting transitions between hues of Crantini, Cassis, Kryptonite, Bellini, Hypnotic and Martini at the flick of a switch.

LEFT The geometrically ingenious kitchen welcomes eastern waterfront vistas.

ABOVE The coloured LED lighting in the upper glass cabinets creates dynamic atmospheric changes.

RIGHT The interplay between the artworks – the bronze paneled mural and the intense colour of the triptych – enriches the dining experience.

LEFT The penthouse's spaciousness showcases the spectacular southern views.

RIGHT The state of the art entertainment area opens up to an illuminated bar.

Q
The
Quintessential
Dry Gin
level

The reflective resin countertop of the bar and the extended compound curved wall allow easy passage to the master suite.

LEFT The 38th floor master bedroom overlooks the city's north shore.

ABOVE The walk-through dressing area complements the ambience of the master en suite.

RIGHT The master en suite boasts a luxurious spa and steam shower with an inspiring view of English Bay.

CHATEAU GRANVILLE
HOT L

PREVIOUS PAGE Shimmering city lights overlook the northwest mountains and English Bay.

LEFT This penthouse features expansive views overlooking Yaletown, maximized by dramatic double height living.

RIGHT Warmth and intimacy is created by sculptural lighting.

LEFT This residence's open spaces with select materials assuring visual continuity throughout.

ABOVE L.E.D. lighting emphasizes the strong directional elements.

RIGHT An open-plan kitchen with simple forms and clean lines harmonizes adjacent living spaces.

PREVIOUS PAGE LEFT A dynamic spiral steel staircase and curved kitchen bar maximize flow and openness.

PREVIOUS PAGE RIGHT Translucent glass doors, honed granite floor and the zebrawood wall paneling are subdued by coloured L.E.D. lighting.

LEFT The ergonomic comfort of a desk's curvature contrasts with the rectangular, full-height zebrawood finishes of the millwork.

CENTRE Zebrawood cabinetry adds texture and warmth against the coolness of the white porcelain trough sink.

RIGHT A glowing ambiance is created by illuminating the translucent bench in the steam shower.

LEFT An ensuite mini bar adds stylish convenience.

RIGHT Floor to ceiling glass sheeting divides the state-of-the-art ensuite spa and master bedroom. Hard surfaces are softened by luxurious hotel style bedding.

Richard Salter Diane Salter

Richard & Diane Salter RICHARD SALTER INTERIORS LTD

Form follows function – style follows beauty, and for Richard and Diane Salter, the design is in the details.

The Salters embrace the opportunity to create interiors that are truly original, maintaining an understanding of the client and their needs. Following in the footsteps of the great West Coast architects, these homes offer international styling in harmony with the natural elements. Rectangular elements define space and balance, assimilating the play of angles – deliberate and architectural – studies in subtraction with floating elements, some dissolving while others remain.

True to form, the outdoors is invited in. Light flows through windows which perfectly frame the outdoor panorama – sky, mountains and sea. In the selection of materials for the interior – warm translates to wood, stone and fire, and cold to glass and water – all presented with unblemished continuity. Each distinctive interior allows for the flow of patterns and rhythms of life.

The Salters' homes are intelligently designed with an uncomplicated aesthetic that makes them highly pleasurable to live in. The use of colour is synchronized by elemental patterns in wood grains, fabrics and tiles – nature's textures applied to clean architectural definition. These exquisite homes are contemporary and timeless, presented with architectural integrity and meticulously executed details.

The Salter's signature is sophisticated style that is enriched by the splendour of nature. In balance, both inside and out.

PREVIOUS PAGE Breathtaking vistas of North Shore and Gulf Islands. The finest in West Coast living is offered by the architectural elegance and international style of this residence.

LEFT The bold forms and refined lines of the living room fireplace restate the simplicity of structure.

RIGHT A two-way limestone fireplace in the foyer leads into the dining room. A private art collection is framed by interior detailing. An elegant entryway and dining area feature artistic structural elements. McGuire chairs surround an Armani dining table, creating a fusion of Asian and contemporary lines.

LEFT An outdoor space is warmed by a fireplace seamlessly integrated with the interior.

RIGHT The sliding open doors unify the continuity of the indoor/outdoor relationship and maximize ocean views.

LEFT Positive and negative forms are exposed by the family room's fireplace, complementing the art collection.

RIGHT The family room contains a synergy of materials and textures adding visual interest. Italian furnishings, accessories and art complement the interior architecture.

LEFT This centrally located kitchen features a sophisticated synthesis of materials – graphite coloured lacquer, natural maple and granite.

RIGHT A negative edge pool designed by architect Mike Kaffka ensures the continuity of the elements and the water views beyond.

Rob Blaney FX-40 BUILDING DESIGN

"It's about who the clients are, not about who I am." To this end, Blaney's goal is to give them what they want – interiors that are a reflection of their lifestyle and personal experiences. His willingness to explore innovative design possibilities delivers his modern interiors with distinctive flair.

Blaney finds that his client's involvement inspires his own creativity as a designer. The dynamics of the design process is fueled by his client's enthusiasm. His challenge is to create spaces that allow the homeowner to experience a sense of renewal and excitement in their newly discovered environment.

"I would live in a glass house if I could," says Blaney, who has a passion for glass. It reminds him of water in nature and its inherent calming and soothing quality. Elemental materials – glass and water, natural rock, wood and metal, earth tones – are integrated in his interiors producing homes that are organically at one with nature.

With an intuitive appreciation for natural light, he designs spaces that allow for as much light as possible. In addition, he incorporates the greenery of the surrounding landscape, while maximizing privacy. Integrated with the neighbourhood and the surrounding natural environment, these residences echo Blaney's essential approach to design.

As a minimalist, Blaney interprets the architecture as the frame for the interior structure, and its furniture as the statement. He mixes dynamic visual and tactile elements that are adaptable to the homeowner's evolving lifestyle.

Blaney's signature is modern – exploring the world's cultures and influences in contemporary design, while creating excitement in the process.

PREVIOUS PAGE A sophisticated Yaletown living room features cheerful amber leather furnishings and dark brown Sambuca flooring. The geodesic dome of Science World beckons in the distance.

LEFT A directional flooring inlay of Quartlite granite and Sambuca hardwood surrounds an elliptical kitchen isle.

RIGHT The pathway of the dramatic arc leads to the dining room on one side and to the bedrooms on the other. A hallway mirror gallery adds dimension.

PREVIOUS PAGE LEFT A series of floor-to-ceiling wood frame mirror panels expand the narrow hallway. The strategic floor inlay re-proportions the dimensions of the passageway.

PREVIOUS PAGE CENTRE In the entry, a balanced composition of vertical and horizontal wood grains and stainless steel sets the stage for the sophisticated theme.

PREVIOUS PAGE RIGHT Wall-to-wall-mirrors expand the width of the narrow interior. The curve of the open kitchen isle is sculpted in dark walnut and stainless steel.

LEFT The deluxe master bedroom rests under a bowed dropped ceiling canopy.

ABOVE The elements of nature are heightened by the contrast of alabaster flowers displayed against the dark wood finishes.

RIGHT The strategic use of curvatures and mirrors circulate throughout this sophisticated residence.

Miele

Barbara Houston HOUSTON & ASSOCIATES

With her feet planted firmly on the ground and her dreams in full colour, the designs of Barbara Houston embrace the intrinsic relationship between the simplicity of the earth's elements and the incredibly clear human scale we apply to the spaces we live in.

Urban living necessitates a place to call home. Houston's urban sanctuaries offer an oasis of serenity, evoking the sublime and giving a deep breath to space – open to the energy of the city outside within the framework of excellent home design.

For Houston, deconstruction begins the process. She finds inspiration and excitement in the exploration of using materials differently than their original intention – the discomfort of flipping floor plans horizontally or vertically that may lead to a transformation of the space. This exploration often results in unearthing how the space works best through the energy of constant evolution.

The ocean is her prairie, the mountains her sky, and the design aesthetic is all about long, low and beautiful plains. Views and vistas are discovered with an innate understanding of the quality of light and an extraordinary ability to manipulate volumes – to enhance the perception.

Houston addresses the space we live in simply – the walls are the artist's canvas and the people who live there are the colour. Houston's design palette is muted and neutral, allowing objects d'art their strong, vibrant colours to live at high intensity. Floors ground us, concrete or grey surfaces are preferred media for representing the earth – a reminder of our essential bond to the natural world.

Houston's signature is innovative solutions and inspiring designs that produce successful and exceptional homes.

PREVIOUS PAGE East of the city, 4th Avenue abounds with city view lofts. Strategically defined rooms are grounded with mahogany. White-on-white tones expand the living space.

LEFT An efficient central fireplace with volumetric and planar spatial connectors links to the mezzanine.

RIGHT Planar elements in multiple layers and a frameless glass panel create an amplitude of visual interest.

A meditative loft sleeping area offers quiet relaxation.

LEFT A subtle ceiling aperture invites moonlight bathing in the Sybaritic soaker tub, complete with a glass paneled wall and rainfall shower.

RIGHT A self-contained sleeping and bathing area is situated in the upper-most flyover.

Thu Watson TRUE WORTH REALTY CORP.

In the world of distinctive interiors Thu Watson is noteworthy by designing many of Vancouver's high-end residential and commercial properties.

For Watson, it begins with a clarity of vision resulting in luxurious interior spaces. Her reverence to Vancouver's signature as the highest quality of life is showcased at the top echelon – the top of residential skyscrapers with breathtaking views of the city, mountains and ocean. Her ultra modern penthouses are sought after by a sophisticated international clientèle.

Exclusive turnkey design is her forté – contemporary interiors reflecting the harmonious balance of beauty and the implicit order of the surrounding natural elements. Each interior encompasses echoes of stone and water, cold and warm, light and dark, smooth and textured, wood and metal, streamlined curves, strength and sensuality.

An idealist with an intrinsic aesthetic sense, Watson's designs seamlessly embrace both comfort and luxury. She creates dynamic spaces where no surface is overlooked, from cool painted glass walls and sculpted waterfalls to exotic wood paneled walls and fireplaces. Mirrors reflect and expand spaciousness, enhancing the aesthetic of the sumptuous décor and the exquisite European furnishings.

Expect the unexpected – eye catching enchanting design revelations. Each interior mirrors her personal philosophy of living well – living spaces that are stylish and sexy, but equally luxurious and inviting. For Watson, home is a reflection of the world outside and her offering to the homeowner is a sense of uniquely personal residence. She believes that a well-designed interior has positive influences on its resident's quality of life; accordingly she delivers a lasting bequest of order and beauty.

The fait accompli of Watson's signature is the satisfying sensation of being at the very apex of the world reveling in elegance, contemporary style and sophistication.

PREVIOUS PAGE This elegant Yaletown penthouse offers the best of West Coast living. A sophisticated residence complete with cosmopolitan amenities. Endless recreational possibilities are close at hand – David Lam Park, Vancouver's celebrated Seawall and False Creek Ferries to Granville Island. Diverse urban living.

LEFT An inviting vestibule is furnished with a stately armoire, expertly niched in the alcove of a formerly traditional closet.

RIGHT Open spaces surrounded by exotic wood echo the distant forests. A delicate chandelier mimics the glistening city lights.

LEFT Objects d'art – sculptures in the form of furniture, illumination, paintings and music – graciously revealed in every room.

RIGHT This exotic interior is characterized by tropical floral arrangements – lilies, anthirium, orchids and bamboo.

LEFT A console table of rippled glass and mahogany flooring, echoes of nature itself.

ABOVE Works by local artists are expertly exhibited in a galleria along an interior hallway.

LEFT Horizontal wood panels with stainless groove insets clad the floor-to-ceiling height fireplace of this contemporary dining room.

RIGHT Indoor comfort extends to the outdoor terrace for elegant moonlight dining.

PREVIOUS PAGE LEFT A Roche Bobois shelving unit displays earthy materials of leather and wood.

PREVIOUS PAGE CENTRE A free standing wall of bamboo offers residents daytime privacy.

PREVIOUS PAGE RIGHT The understated master bedroom – thoughtfully designed for resting luxuriously.

NEXT PAGE Yaletown at night. Dazzling lights illuminate the pulse of one of the world's most exciting cities.

MEREDITH
Eclectic Style

PREVIOUS PAGE LEFT A structural column transformed into a three-sided rippled glass waterfall. High drama is achieved by the contrast of the white leather sofa against the dark Wenge flooring.

PREVIOUS PAGE RIGHT Vertical rippled glass panels emulate water, subtle back lighting adds depth.

LEFT A myriad of shimmering surfaces – lacquered kitchen cabinets, polished granite, back painted glass wall panels, mirrors and stainless steel, grounded by the wood floors and doors.

RIGHT The kitchen cabinets are innovatively designed with a tambour garage to conceal small appliances.

LEFT An illuminated silver leaf architectural dome dominates the ceiling of this elegant dining room. A delicate chandelier lends a whimsical atmosphere.

CENTRE A two-tier contemporary teacart serves as a butler by offering cocktails.

RIGHT Back painted glass paneled corridor leads to the master bedroom, featuring custom double doors with half moon opaque glass inserts.

FAR LEFT A meditative seating area features luscious fabrics. Sophisticated tranquility.

LEFT The master bedroom expresses strength and sensuality with sumptuous décor. A dropped ceiling bed canopy conforms to the contour of the soaker tub.

RIGHT An upholstered headboard clad behind cabinet partitions the master suite from the bathroom.

FAR RIGHT The ensuite bathroom resembles an undersea fantasy complete with aqua glass wall panels, Cerulean-blue floor tiles, and vessel sinks – alive with underwater hues of aquamarine, tangerine and crimson.

GIORGIO ARMANI

Mitchell Freedland MITCHELL FREEDLAND DESIGNS

A celebrated reputation has made Freedland eminent in the realm of Western Canada's finest homes and developments, as well as internationally. Mentioning an interior design by Mitchell Freedland evokes a vision of cool contemporary ingenuity defined by clean, tailored lines.

There is a sense of the enigmatic that emanates from Freedland's designs. Mixing a simple cohesive palette with dramatic lighting sets the stage for entertaining or simply enjoying the pleasures of home. He invites the challenge of small condominiums, for they engage the mind to redefine logistics for designing tight spaces.

The art of illusion and reflection, achieved by accentuated long lines, highlights the flexibility of the space rather than emphasizing its confinement. The reassuring tone-on-tone of rich neutrals opens and expands the rooms as the warm wood accents strengthen and ground the high-risen abodes. The sense of space allows one to savour the colours and textures while appreciating the innovative space enhancements.

The residences designed by Freedland maintain a fine balance between design and comfort within the urban landscape. From entertaining spaces to an intimate retreat – each home is a refined place to relax, connect and live, simply and elegantly.

Freedland's signature is his distinctive design aesthetic that emits its eloquent statement in any cosmopolitan environment.

PREVIOUS PAGE Coal Harbour – A cosmopolitan lifestyle within minutes of Vancouver's vibrant downtown core, world-class restaurants, fabulous shopping and the inner harbour. A balance of refined aesthetics, natural beauty and urban sophistication in one of the world's most dynamic cities.

LEFT The sensuous oval curves of the dropped ceiling and mahogany dining table define the elegant dining area from the tailored family room. Recessed lighting creates a sublime atmosphere.

RIGHT Stone and glass are harmoniously juxtaposed in a glass-enclosed powder room.

LEFT An open-concept kitchen blends effortlessly with the living/dining area. Rich mahogany completes the balance.

RIGHT An oversized island serves dual purpose for casual or large-scale entertaining.

GIORGIO ARMANI

LEFT A deluxe master bedroom wrapped in sensual textures and effusive hues, illuminated by ambient lighting and a glowing fire.

ABOVE The ensuite walls feature back painted glass and tailored detailing, balancing the contrasting materials of mahogany and limestone.

RIGHT The master suite is furnished with custom-designed Macassar ebony night stands.

The indoor/outdoor design of this residence offers a sophisticated urban enclave with easy access to Vancouver's vibrant city scene, and the West Coast's natural bounty beyond.

Thu Watson TRUE WORTH REALTY CORP.

David Christopher FX-40 BUILDING DESIGN

When two creative minds such as Thu Watson and David Christopher collaborate in the design of an interior, there is no limit to the heights they can achieve. There's a tangible synergy between Christopher's sense of adventure in design and Watson's clarity of vision that culminates in an exceptional result.

The fusion of their individual talents have merited them the honourable designation for the cover of *Vancouver Signature Interiors*. The unique fusion of these two masters of design elevates Vancouver's international design profile.

Sharing ideas and design ideals allows the vision to expand and the design adventure to be fueled by creative energy. Once the adventure begins, they consult with each other every step of the way, from selecting fine materials and finishes to defining an exquisite colour palette that will enhance the overall design. In unison they set the stage for a truly world-class interior.

With feminine force and masculine strength designing in tandem, their sensual and powerful interiors celebrate *la difference*.

Watson and Christopher – their signature is vision and adventure à deux that soars.

PREVIOUS PAGE Visionary living above the skyline. A spectacular Yaletown penthouse overlooks the International Quayside Marina in False Creek. This impeccably detailed kitchen was inspired by a top-of-the-line automobile. The integrated cabinets and adjacent hallway paneling surfaces are styled in Aston Martin automotive metallic paint.

LEFT A spiral staircase trimmed in stainless steel – a structural sculpture featuring individually lit wooden treads. A gallery of paintings exhibits local artist Ronan Boyle's work.

ABOVE Dropped ceilings juxtapose in three tiers, each featuring a guiding light scheme that draws the eyes to the breathtaking views. A Mylar clad ceiling reflects the yachts of the Quayside Marina below.

RIGHT The dining room is expertly designed for elegant entertaining. A dramatic dance of the elements – shimmering fire, enchanting lights and a glass encased waterfall.

PREVIOUS PAGE LEFT The home office features a stainless steel clad column. A discreet private doorway leads to a curved nautical-inspired balcony.

PREVIOUS PAGE RIGHT In the guest bedroom, continuity is maintained between the darkness of the wood floor and the custom built-in wardrobe.

LEFT Coved L.E.D. lighting casts a subdued ambiance in the master bedroom.

CENTRE Drama is created in an opened ensuite spa by juxtaposing pistachio back-painted glass panels and Absolute black granite slab.

RIGHT The luxurious master bedroom redefines the meaning of living well – a Dolce Vita lounge chair, an exotic orchid arrangement – sophisticated pleasures.

SLINGSBY

LEFT An upper loft overlooks the sumptuous living room, leading to an outdoor cedar deck. A painting by local artist Tanya Slingsby.

RIGHT The roof deck's landing offers some of the most spectacular views of Pacific Ocean sunsets — a soothing respite.

ACKNOWLEDGEMENTS

INTERIORS

Robert Blaney
FX-40 Building Design Corp.
TEL 604.922.6092
info@fx40.com
www.fx40.com

David Christopher
FX-40 Building Design Corp.
TEL 604.922.6092
info@fx40.com
www.fx40.com

Ted Feenstra
Feenstra Architecture Inc
ted@feenstra.ca
TEL 604.739.8888

Mitchell Freedland
Mitchell Freedland Design
TEL 604.733.3600
www.mitchellfreedland.com

Barbara Houston
Barbara Houston Design Inc
TEL 604.806.0281

Robert Ledingham
Ledingham Design Consultants
TEL 604.874.4900
info@ledingham.com
www.ledingham.com

Alda Pereira
Alda Pereira Design
TEL 604.736.2179
alda@telus.net
www.aldapereiradesign.com

Richard & Diane Salter
Richard Salter Interiors Ltd
TEL 604.730.9220

Thu Watson
True Worth Realty Corp.
TEL 604.232.4059
thu@trueworthrealty.com
www.trueworthrealty.com

PUBLISHER

Thu Watson
True Worth Realty Corp.
120-8211 Sea Island Way
Richmond, BC V6X 7W3
TEL 604.232.4059
thu@trueworthrealty.com
www.trueworthrealty.com

PROJECT MANAGER

Marc LaBrie
TEL 604.616.4704
marc@marclabrie.com
www.marclabrie.com

EDITOR

Lorraine Demers
TEL 604.722.2977
ldid@novuscom.net

ART DIRECTOR / DESIGNER

Todd Chapman
Hangar 18 Creative Group Inc.
TEL 604.737.7111
www.hangar18creative.com

CONTRIBUTING WRITERS

Tracey Ellis

Gwendolyn Gawlick
TEL 604.716.8243
gg@prdiva.com
www.prdiva.com

Sherry Matthews
TEL 778.998.5759
slmatthews@shaw.ca

DISTRIBUTOR

18 KARAT
TEL 1.888.849.8811
FAX 604.856.8305
info@eighteenkarat.com

PRINT COORDINATOR

Matthew Toren
TEL 604.782.4810

PHOTOGRAPHY INTERIORS

Ivan Hunter
Ivan Hunter Photography
TEL 604.739.2008
ivan@ivanhunter.com
www.ivanhunter.com

Ivan Hunter grew up in Victoria, British Columbia, in a house designed by his father. Photographs of great architecture coupled with the ambience of the west coast and Japanese culture, engendered in him an early affinity for environmental concerns and the importance of craft in daily life.

At the age of 18 Ivan began his photographic career on a tour of Asia and Europe, and later received a Bachelor of Arts degree from the Brooks Institute of Photography. His belief is that architectural space is successfully photographed only through the careful control of detailed relationships.

PHOTOGRAPHY PORTRAITS

Robert Kent
Robert Kent Photography
TEL 604.736.8066
niki@robertkentphoto.com
www.robertkentphoto.com www.compassionateeye.org

The rk studio is proud founder of the compassionate eye foundation, an innovative non profit organization based out of Vancouver, BC. We are a group of photographers and creative professionals committed to giving back. Our goal is to support, honour and empower those in developing nations in order to expand their possibilities for sustainable development.

A portion of Robert Kent's creative fees are donated to the compassionate eye foundation.

We extend our appreciation to the amazing homeowners for opening their doors to the world.

VANCOUVER *Signature* INTERIORS